Otto

Welcome t[...]

Family from all at

St. Mary's, Beaconsfield.

AF281004

My Big Story Bible

CANDLE
BOOKS

Copyright © 2015 Lion Hudson/Tim Dowley Associates Ltd

All rights reserved. No part of this publication may be reproduced or transmitted in any form or by any means, electronic or mechanical, including photocopy, recording, or any information storage and retrieval system, without permission in writing from the publisher.

Published by Candle Books
an imprint of
Lion Hudson plc
Wilkinson House, Jordan Hill Road,
Oxford OX2 8DR, England
www.lionhudson.com/candle

ISBN 978 1 78128 203 8
e-ISBN 978 1 78128 239 7

First edition 2015

Acknowledgments
The Lord's Prayer on page 62 is adapted from the Good News Bible
© 1994 published by the Bible Societies/HarperCollins Publishers Ltd UK,
Good News Bible © American Bible Society 1966, 1971, 1976, 1992.
Used with permission.

A catalogue record for this book is available from the British Library

Printed and bound in Malaysia, April 2015, LH18

My
BIG
STORY BIBLE

by Josh Edwards
illustrated by Christine Tappin

CONTENTS

NEW TESTAMENT

OLD TESTAMENT

IN THE BEGINNING

In the beginning,
God made heaven and earth.
God said, "Let there be light!"
And there was light.
God put water in the sea
and clouds in the sky.
He made mountains,
hills, and valleys.
And God saw it was all good.

How many different flowers can you see in the picture?

GOD MAKES PEOPLE

Then God created the first man, Adam,
and the first woman, Eve.
He made them like himself
so they could be his friends.
God gave Adam and Eve a beautiful garden.
It was called the Garden of Eden.

God told Adam to name the animals.
What names would you have given them?

GOD SAVES NOAH

"A great flood is coming," God told Noah.
"Build a huge boat and fill it
with two of every kind of animal."
Soon the terrible flood came.
But Noah, his family, and all the animals
were kept safe in the ark.
God helped Noah escape the flood.

What did God put in the sky when the great flood was over?

Abraham Moves Home

Long ago, in a far-off land called Ur,
there lived a man named Abraham,
with his wife Sarah.
"Leave your home!" God told Abraham.
"I'm giving you a special new land."
After journeying many months,
Abraham and Sarah came to the land
that God had promised them.
There were lush, green valleys
and fast-flowing rivers.

*Although Sarah was very old, she had a son
named Isaac.*

15

 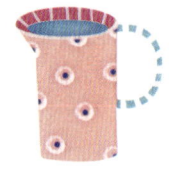 

A WIFE FOR ISAAC

When Isaac grew up he wanted to get married.
Abraham sent a servant to find his son a wife.
"Choose the woman who gives you
water for your camels!" God told him.
The servant journeyed many days.
One evening a woman asked him,
"Shall I fetch water for your camels?"
At once the servant knew
this woman should be Isaac's wife.

God helped Isaac find a wife.

THE DREAMTELLER

Joseph was in jail – although he had
done nothing wrong.
In jail he met the king's baker
and the king's servant.
Both of them had very strange dreams.
"Whatever do our dreams mean?"
they asked worriedly.
Joseph told the baker and the servant
just what their dreams meant.

God helped Joseph explain both men's dreams.

SAFE IN A BASKET

Baby Moses' mother was very frightened.
A wicked king was trying to kill baby boys.
So she put her little baby in a basket
and floated it on the river.
Soon the princess came to bathe there.
As soon as she saw the baby, she loved him.
The princess took baby Moses to her palace.
God helped keep Moses safe.

What happened next to Moses?
Let's find out!

21

A BURNING BUSH

When he grew up, Moses ran away
to the desert and became a shepherd.
One day he noticed a bush was on fire.
This bush just kept burning
– it never burned away.
Suddenly a voice called, "Moses!"
"Here I am," Moses answered.
"Take off your sandals!" said the voice.
"The place where you're standing is holy…
I, God, am speaking!"

Then God told Moses to lead his people out of Egypt.

A ROAD ACROSS THE SEA

Moses stood by the deep, wide Red Sea.
His people had to get to the other side.
"Hold up your arms!" God told Moses.
He did – and the waters parted.
Moses led his people across the seabed.
Then the waters fell back.
The soldiers chasing them couldn't follow.
God saved his people.

Moses rescued his people from the king of Egypt.

24

GOD'S LAWS

Now Moses led his people into the desert.
One day they arrived at a high mountain.
Moses climbed the mountain
and met with God there.
God gave him two great stones.
On the stones he wrote God's
ten special rules for living.

We often call these rules the Ten Commandments.

CROSSING THE RIVER

At last God's people reached the River Jordan.
On the other side was the land
that God had promised them.
"Step into the water!" said God.
"Carry the Holy Ark across."
They did, and a dry pathway opened up.
Soon everyone was safely over.
Now God's people had entered
the Promised Land!

God had promised this land to his people many years before.

A CITY COLLAPSES

Joshua was the new leader of God's people.
He took them to the great city of Jericho.
"March your army around the walls
seven times," God told Joshua.
"Then blow your trumpets
– and everyone shout very loud!"
They did – and the walls fell.
God helped Joshua destroy this mighty city.

Guess what their trumpets were made of!

VERY LONG HAIR

Among God's people there was a boy
named Samson.
He never, ever cut his hair!
He grew it very, very long to show
that he was doing special work for God.
Samson grew up to be a mighty strong man.
One day he killed a lion with his bare hands.
Samson knew God gave him this strength.

Would you like to grow your hair really long?

THE BOY WHO HELPED

Hannah prayed, "Please Lord, give me a son!
When he grows up, he can help
in your holy tent."
Before long, Hannah did have a baby.
She named him Samuel.
When he was old enough, she took him
to the high priest.
"I have brought my son Samuel
to help you," she told him.

What's inside the holy tent?

GOD CHOOSES A KING

Samuel grew up to become a great leader.
One day God sent him to find a new king.
He visited a man who had many sons.
But none of them was quite right.
"Do you have any more sons?" asked Samuel.
"There's young David," said the father.
"But he's just a shepherd boy."
"Send for him!" said Samuel.
When David came, God told Samuel,
"*This* young man will be the next king of Israel."

David could play the harp beautifully.

DAVID BEATS A GIANT

There lived a giant bully called Goliath.
None of God's people wanted to fight him.
"I will fight this giant!" said little David.
He used just his shepherd's sling.
David carefully chose a stone then flung it.
It struck the giant and he fell to the ground.
Crash! Wallop! Thud!
God helped David beat the mighty giant.

David became the greatest king of God's people.

A TEMPLE FOR GOD

King Solomon built a beautiful temple
where his people could sing and pray.
When it was finished,
priests carried the Holy Ark inside.
The Temple filled with dazzling light
to show that God was with his people.
"Lord, hear our prayers!" said Solomon.

Solomon became famous because he was very, very wise.

A CAPTAIN IS HEALED

Naaman was a brave soldier.
But he had a nasty skin disease called leprosy.
"Elisha's God could help you," said his maid.
So Naaman went to visit Elisha.
"Go, wash in the river seven times!" said Elisha.
"*Then* you'll be well."
Naaman dipped in the river –
once, twice, three times…
The seventh time, the leprosy vanished!
God had healed him.

Do you think Naaman thanked his maid when he got home?

SAVED FROM LIONS

Daniel prayed three times every day.
Until one day the king said, "*No one* must pray.
Anyone who does will be thrown to the lions."
But Daniel kept on praying to God.
So the king threw Daniel in the lions' pit.
God's angel shut the hungry lions' mouths.
God helped keep Daniel safe from the lions.

After this, the king said everyone *should pray to God!*

A FISH RESCUES JONAH

Jonah was running away from God.
He went to a port and sailed off in a boat.
Suddenly a fierce storm blew.
The sailors flung Jonah into the waves.
Before he could drown, a great fish swallowed
him. Jonah lived inside that fish for three days.
Then it spat him out on the seashore.
God saved Jonah from drowning.

After this, Jonah never *ran away*
from God again!

47

NEW TESTAMENT

THE FIRST CHRISTMAS

One day an angel suddenly appeared to Mary.
"You will have a special baby," he told her.
"You must call him Jesus!"
Mary was really, really happy.
With her husband Joseph,
she started to get ready for the baby.
But first they had to go on a long,
tiring journey to the town of Bethlehem.

Where would they stay in Bethlehem?

No Room

When they arrived, Bethlehem was very busy.
There was no room for them at the inn.
But the kind innkeeper said,
"You can sleep in my little stable."
And there, in the borrowed stable,
Mary's baby was born.
She named him "Jesus".

Why did Mary call her baby "Jesus"?

WISE MEN SEARCH

Some wise men were watching the night sky.
Suddenly they noticed a bright, new star.
"That means a new king is born,"
they said. "Let's follow the star!"
The wise men journeyed many miles.
Finally the star stopped over Bethlehem.
There the wise men found baby Jesus.
They gave him rich presents.

The wise men gave Jesus gold, and rich scents
called frankincense and myrrh.

JESUS HELPS

Mary and Joseph took Jesus back home
with them to the village of Nazareth.
Joseph was a carpenter.
Jesus helped him saw wood and hammer nails.
Jesus also helped his mother
and played with his friends.
The village teacher taught him to read.
Jesus was getting ready for the work
that God wanted him to do.

Do you help your mum and dad?

57

JOHN BAPTIZES JESUS

Jesus' cousin, John, lived in the desert.
One day when Jesus had grown up,
he went to see John.
"Please baptize me!" said Jesus.
So John dipped Jesus in the River Jordan.
As Jesus came out of the water,
a dove flew above him.
"This is my Son," said a voice.
"I am very pleased with him!"

Who do you think was speaking?

JESUS PICKS A TEAM

Now Jesus was ready to begin
his special work for God.
He needed to pick a team of helpers.
First he chose four fishermen.
Then he saw a man called Matthew
collecting tax money.
"Leave your job," said Jesus.
"Follow me!" And he did.

Altogether Jesus chose 12 special friends.
We often call them his "disciples".

HOW TO PRAY

One of Jesus' friends asked,
"How should we pray?"
So Jesus taught them:

Our Father in heaven,
May your holy name be respected;
May your kingdom come;
May your will be done on earth,
as it is in heaven.
Give us today the food we need.
Forgive us the wrongs we have done,
As we forgive the wrongs
that others have done to us.
Do not bring us to temptation,
But keep us safe from evil.

We often call this "The Lord's Prayer".

A SUDDEN STORM

One day Jesus was sailing with his friends.
He was very tired and soon fell fast asleep.
All of a sudden a great storm blew.
Jesus' friends felt very scared.
"Jesus, *wake up*!" they shouted.
"We're all going to drown."
"Storm – be quiet!" Jesus ordered.
Immediately everything was calm again.
Jesus helped his friends when they were scared.

Even the wind and waves listened to Jesus!

THE KIND STRANGER

This is one of Jesus' special stories.

A man was walking along a lonely road.
Suddenly thieves beat him up and robbed him.
A priest saw him, but just walked on.
A helper from the Temple also walked by.
But a kind stranger stopped and helped him.
"Which of these men was a *true* friend?" asked Jesus.
"The stranger!" people replied.
"Treat everyone you meet the same way," said Jesus.

We often call this the story of the Good Samaritan.

THE GOOD SHEPHERD

Jesus told this great story too.

There was once a shepherd who had 100 sheep.
"One of my sheep is missing," said the
shepherd one night. "I must go and find it."
After a long search, the shepherd found
his lost sheep. He carried it home.
"Be happy!" he told his friends.
"I've found my lost sheep."
"I am just like a good shepherd," said Jesus.

Why do you think Jesus is like a good shepherd?

THE TWO HOUSES

Jesus told this story as well.

Once two men each decided to build a house.
The first man built on sand.
The second built on hard rock.
As soon as they had finished, a storm broke.
CRRRAASHH!!!
The first man's house soon fell flat!
But the second man's house stood firm.
"People who listen to my words and act on them," said Jesus, "are like the man who built his house on rock."

What's happening to the house built on sand?

70

PRAISE GOD

Jesus brought his friends to Jerusalem
for the great festival.
He borrowed a donkey and rode into the city.
People were very pleased to see him.
They waved palm-tree leaves and shouted,
"Praise God! *Hooray* for God!"

We remember this special day on Palm Sunday.

Jesus' Last Supper

It was time for the great feast.
Jesus' twelve special friends ate supper
with him in an upstairs room.
"Love one another, as I love you!" Jesus said.
He took the bread, broke it,
and gave some to his friends.
Then Jesus took a cup of wine.
He passed it to his disciples.

Jesus told his friends sadly that he was going to die soon.

A VERY SAD DAY

Cruel soldiers marched Jesus to a hill.
There they put him on a wooden cross.
They put a robber on a cross
on each side of him.
But Jesus had done *nothing* wrong.
The sky went very dark and he died.
Jesus' family and friends watched sadly.
A good man put Jesus' body in a grave.

Is this the end of the story?

JESUS IS ALIVE

Forty days later, Jesus' friends were together.
Suddenly Jesus appeared to them.
"Don't be afraid!" said Jesus. "Men killed me
– but God brought me back to life."
Then Jesus took his friends up a hill.
"Now I am going to be with God," he said.
"But I'm still with you. I *always* will be."
Then a cloud took Jesus away.

*Jesus said, "Go and tell this good news
to everyone in the world!"*

I Lov U

You